Skegness

IN OLD PHOTOGRAPHS

Skegness lifeboat *Anne Allan* towing the sailing yacht *FLB* into the Haven at Gibraltar Point in the late 1930s, after she had been in trouble in the Wash. The initials FLB stood for 'fine little boat'.

Skegness

IN OLD PHOTOGRAPHS

Collected by WINSTON KIME

Alan Sutton Publishing Limited
Phoenix Mill · Far Thrupp · Stroud
Gloucestershire

First published 1992

British Library Cataloguing in Publication Data
Kime, Winston
Skegness in Old Photographs
I. Title
942.532

ISBN 0–7509–0121–7

Typeset in 9/10 Sabon.
Typesetting and origination by
Alan Sutton Publishing Limited.
Printed in Great Britain by
The Bath Press, Avon.

Contents

A 1928 view of North Parade from the Pier ramp.

Introduction

Seaside resorts have been particularly well served by picture postcard manufacturers, as the holidaymaker's 'wish you were here' greeting to friends and relatives has been almost a ritual for the last century. The picture postcard has helped the cause of historical topography and architecture, but it only occasionally gets to the real heart of community life. For that, we have to rely on local photographers, professional and amateur. Many of their faded prints now reside in family albums or have been pushed away in drawers and almost forgotten, and, too often, they finish up in rubbish bags when the owner dies. Thankfully, as I have found in compiling this book, a lot of individuals do preserve and pass down some of these photos of people and places of long ago. Most of us enjoy a tot of nostalgia; it can take us back to when we were young, or open a door on a world we never knew.

The earliest known professional photographer in Skegness was Charles Smyth, who was established in High Street in 1882. He later moved into the new Lumley Road and, during the summer, he also had a seafront studio in a wooden hut on the south side of the Clock Tower. He was also, for many years, choirmaster of the Wesleyan Chapel.

Samuel Charles Burnham had another wooden studio, on the north side of the Pier, from the 1890s until his death in 1913. Alfred Wrate set up his business at 17 Lumley Road in 1907, and it was the most successful photography firm in Skegness for more than half the present century. He died in middle age and the business was continued by his widow and family until they ceased trading in 1982, the photographic works and shop having moved to the east end of Lumley Road in the early 1930s.

Walking snapshots became popular at the seaside just after the First World War, and Mrs Amelia Wrate was soon leading the field at Skegness and opening branches at Mablethorpe and Sutton-on-Sea. Young men and girls in bright orange striped blazers caught the trippers on the parades and esplanades, snapping hundreds a day with their handy little cameras, and the prints were ready a few hours later.

Perhaps the earliest Skegness practitioner of this type of photography, however, was Mr Snaps himself, alias Bert Jackson, who began on the Pier in 1920. His later spot in Butlin's nearby amusement park was afterwards replaced by Walter Chapman's Corner Studio, while Jack Tansey acquired Snaps Corner in Lumley Road when Jackson moved to Blackpool. But Wrates kept ahead of the competition until the trade declined in the 1960s, probably because by that time many of the visitors came armed with their own small cameras.

Photographers looking for ancient buildings in Skegness could be rather disappointed, as the sum total amounts to two churches, three eighteenth-century farmhouses, and an inn dating from around 1770. The former Skegness parish church of St Clement's, and St Mary's at Winthorpe are both listed Grade II buildings, as are the three farmhouses comprising Church Farm (now the county council's Church Farm Museum), the other Church Farm, near Winthorpe church, and Ivy House on Burgh Road, nearly opposite the football ground. The early nineteenth-century Burn's Farm (listed as Burnside) on Wainfleet Road is also a Grade II building. Burn's Farm and the nearby Church Farm were for many years occupied by the brothers Charles and John Burn respectively. Church Farm at Winthorpe, built in 1765, has belonged to the Tagg family for several generations. The Taggs were also the last to farm at the Church Farm Museum.

The Clock Tower, the Pier, and Coastguard Cottages in St Andrew's Drive complete the town's listed buildings at the time of writing. Rather surprisingly, the eighteenth-century Vine Hotel is not listed, apparently because of subsequent additions and alterations. The Vine's connection with Alfred, Lord Tennyson may be rather tenuous, but it is historically closely bound up with the early bathing-place of Skegness. It is unfortunate that the Tennysons' Skegness lodgings, the Moat House in Drummond Road, was demolished in the 1890s by the over-enthusiastic builders of the new resort town.

In spite of the dearth of ancient relics, Skegness has been at least a small mark on the map since before Domesday Book. Its name derives from the Scandinavian – redolent of the Viking invasions – *Skeggi*, or the bearded one's, *ness*, or headland, which sheltered the small port. A storm flood, supposedly in 1526, changed the shape of this part of the Lincolnshire coast and the protecting ridge of dunes (the 'ness'), as well as the barrier shoals, were swept away, exposing the town to the full fury of the tide. When the antiquary, John Leland, called here in 1540 he was told that Old Skegness had been 'clene consumid and eten up with the se', and he considered that the rebuilt settlement was but 'a pore new thing'. The inhabitants had salvaged what they could and rebuilt on the new shoreline, half a mile or more inland of the buried haven town.

In 1801 the population was 134, but by 1871, when it had gained a name as a small bathing-place, the figure had swelled to 349. The railway reached Skegness in 1873 and the next census, in 1881, found the population increased by a full thousand. By then, the ninth Earl of Scarbrough, the chief landowner, had decided to diversify because of the agricultural depression and he had created a seaside resort out of what had largely been a small farming and fishing village.

Skegness remained an unpretentious little watering-place until 1922, when the local council purchased the whole of the seashore from Lord Scarbrough at the bargain price of £15,100. The authority then embarked on a development scheme designed to boost it to a place among the leading resorts of the east coast. The basic foreshore layout that we know today was created in the period 1923–37, fifteen years of intensive development transforming what had beenonly sand and dune to a boating lake and bathing pool, esplanades, lawns and rose gardens, ballroom and restaurants, walks and waterway, car parks, bowling greens, and other recreational amenities designed to entice holidaymakers to Skegness. In the post-war years, further improvements have been made and many redundant buildings and businesses have disappeared or changed shape, as we shall see in the following pages.

The summer visitors come to enjoy the sands and sea and the bracing air, and to stroll along the prom-prom-prom where the brass band no longer plays tiddley-om-pom-pom; but there is also a residential town which exists in winter as well as summer and, like inland towns, has a life of its own. There are or have been football and cricket clubs, boys' brigades and girl guides, amateur dramatic and operatic societies, allotment associations and pig clubs, brass bands and dance bands, golf clubs and darts leagues, music associations and bible classes and, in fact, all the sorts of organizations that have flourished in other places all over Britain. You will find pictures of some of these in this book to remind you of what Skegness was like in the years that are gone.

Winston Kime

The Seaside

The seaside up to the middle of the twentieth century was epitomized by deck-chairs, bathing machines, a pier and the donkeys.

44351. *Skegness; Jubilee Clock Tower.* FFACo.

A Francis Frith photograph of 1899 showing the foreshore spreading out to the south of the newly built Clock Tower. The donkey and pony sheds stand on opposite sides of the Lumley Pullover (Tower Esplanade), then comes the museum ship *Eliza*, and a few refreshment huts and stalls, then half a dozen bathing machines near the water's edge. The bare Marine Gardens, with the tall lifeboat flagstaff (a flag was hoisted when the boat was at sea), lie on the seaward side of South Parade, overlooked by the terraces of Victorian boarding houses just off the picture.

Tower Esplanade was in being by 1936, and a prominent feature was the Foreshore Centre, seen above on a day when the lifeboat was on display nearby. It was called the Sands Pavilion when it opened in 1911, but in 1920 it was renamed Café Dansant and advertised 'light luncheons and dainty afternoon teas and an American fountain for iced fruit drinks'. Evening dances and 'tea dances' were held daily in the summer months, and in the wintertime various functions took place there, including Miss Rankin's children's dancing classes on Saturday afternoons. It changed its name again in 1934, this time to the Foreshore Centre, when the District Council's newly formed Foreshore Department established offices there, with other parts of the building used as an information bureau, a lost children's shelter and a first-aid room. The lower picture shows the south side of the Café Dansant in 1928. The building was demolished in 1972.

Until the early part of this century, a helter-skelter and ferris wheel, roundabouts, swing-boats and refreshment huts clustered together on the central beach, just above high-water mark. The ship *Eliza* (below) had been run ashore for breaking up, but Joe Wingate bought the hulk and transformed it into a marine museum featuring a 70 ft whale's skeleton. A high tide in 1911 turned the ship over, causing great damage, and a few months later the contents were dispersed and the wreck was auctioned and sold for £16.

The beach fairground at the bottom of what is now Tower Esplanade in the early 1920s, with Charles Farmer's Midget Photographic Studio on the right.

A studio photograph such as could be obtained from Mr Farmer, although this particular one was made by Charles Smyth at the beginning of the century.

Seats beside the sea were provided for the Edwardian visitors, when pleasure boats abounded and a paddle-steamer ran trips from a landing-stage at the pierhead.

Rowing boats were still doing brisk business in the 1920s, but they disappeared in the years following the Second World War, along with the bathing machines. The horse and cart (seen near the Pier) carried the boat passengers across the creeks at low tide.

Many visitors to the seaside in the 1920s were happy just to sit on the sands and watch the children paddling, or perhaps take a short trip in one of the pleasure boats. Sunshine and sea air sent them home feeling better for the day's outing.

Pleasure boats, with sails rigged, appear to be attracting more spectators than passengers, around 1910.

Moving much faster than the donkeys, the sand yachts of the 1930s could carry several passengers across the firm beach provided there was enough breeze to fill the sails.

In addition to the small rowing and motor boats which operated from the seashore, these two rather grand looking pleasure cruisers ran passenger trips at different periods in the 1930s. The sealbanks in the Wash were a great attraction when, at low tide, scores of seals could be seen basking or flipping about on the exposed shoals. *Royal Lady* has just been loaded from the small boat alongside, but why was she flying the Japanese flag? *Royal Lady* was operated by Fred Fravigar and George Steel.

The *Elizabeth Allan* was named after the Skegness-born film and television star, and was under the command of W.H.R. (Bill) Johnson.

Bathing machines were an integral part of the seaside until the 1950s, allowing the bather to undress inside while being conveyed to the water. At the end of the dip, he or she stepped up the short ladder into the van to be trundled back to the beach. Costumes and towels could be hired from the proprietors who often had lines full, drying in the sun.

Augustine and Frank Fravigar, of Italian descent, came from Boston to sell ice-cream on Skegness beach in 1880, paying half-a-crown a year for their pitch. Augustine's son, with the same name, eventually took over as their ice-cream stalls and barrows began to dot the sands, and in turn his son, Stanley, continued the business until recent times. For many years they manufactured their own product in Alexandra Road. Before cornets and wafers were invented the ice-cream was dispensed in what looked like thick glass egg-cups. This 1920 photograph shows, from left to right, one and a half customers and young Stan Fravigar with his parents, Selina and Augustine II. Mrs Fravigar is standing on a wooden step to serve from the stall. Frank Fravigar's descendents went into manufacturing sweets and now have a large local factory.

Gone paddling, while Mum guards the footwear and baby stays behind to do a bit of spadework, around 1910.

The donkeys are now the oldest attraction on the seashore, and the present day occupants stand waiting for customers just as patiently as these did around 1920, when Tower Esplanade was just a board track across the loose sand.

The Hancocks have been donkeymen on Skegness sands for most of the century, and this 1920 photograph shows 'Knocker' Hancock, far right, and next to him his son, Ben, and two helpers. Ben's son, with the same name, carried on until his retirement a year or so ago.

'Knocker' seems to be coping with two babies, animal and human, in this 1920 snapshot. Lawson's ice-cream kiosk can be seen in the background.

'Knocker' and Ben Hancock compare the luxury of a back seat in a motor car with riding on a donkey.

The elegant Pier entrance of 1881 had what an early Skegness guidebook termed 'two smoothly paved inclines for bath chairs, protected by massive stone balustrades in Roman style'. Sadly, this pleasing balustrading disappeared when the entrance was redesigned in 1936–7. The guidebook also mentioned the striking ornamentation of the gateway buildings. Pictured in 1890, the cobbled strip across the carriageway must have been a very early type of pedestrian crossing, in use long before Hore-Belisha instituted the modern beacon crossings in the 1930s. On the beach, bundles of thorns can be seen half buried to catch the blown sand and form new dunes, while a board walkway led to the sea along what is now Scarbrough Esplanade.

The Victorian Gothic Pier entrance gave way to a contemporary styled replacement in 1937, disposing of the balustrading on the twin ramps. Wrate's Photography occupied one of the shops and pinned their 'walking snaps' along the new wall, where visitors can be seen looking for their pictures. The entrance was rebuilt again in 1972, bringing it down to parade level.

This 1890s crowd near the Pier Hotel may have been watching a carnival procession. The hotel opened in 1881, but was destroyed by fire in 1963, when red brick gave way to a new concrete-faced building on a lower level.

'Peggy' Gadsby was the second one-legged diver to perform from the high-diving board at the end of Skegness Pier. Billy Thomason began in 1904 and Gadsby took over after the First World War. He was followed by his son, 'Daredevil' Leslie, who, although he had two legs, had only one hand having lost the other doing a film stunt. 'Peggy', like Billy Thomason, did a spectacular fire dive from the 90 ft high stage, while Leslie sometimes went off the lower board riding a bicycle or was pushed backwards sitting in a chair. The diving stage was removed in 1949 to make way for a licenced restaurant.

Strolling back from the pierhead in 1922.

'Daredevil' Leslie is pushed off the diving board sitting on a chair.

For many years, horse-drawn landaus took visitors to and from the railway station, on tours around the town, and as far afield as Gibraltar Point. Then came charabancs, buses and taxis, and the trotting horses are now a relic of a bygone age. The landaus lined Tower Esplanade, as did the 'charas', seen below, rival operators vying with one another to take holidaymakers on 'circular tours' at a bob a nob.

Mate's *Illustrated Skegness Guide* of 1903, describing the Pleasure Gardens (now Tower Gardens), said: 'Rustic bowers are conveniently placed for such as seek seclusion and shade from the sun. . . . There is also a pavilion containing dining-rooms, a concert hall and a ballroom. And before the pavilion is a band-stand where orchestral and brass bands occasionally give selections.' The iron bandstand, seldom used in later years, was removed before the Second World War. When the war ended, the pavilion restaurant was operated by the Council's Catering Department for several seasons, and then became an auctioneer's saleroom.

The *Gleaner*, one of two gravel boats which caried gravel from the shingle beaches of Heacham and Snettisham across the Wash to Wainfleet Haven and Skegness, where the cargo was usually dumped near the Sea View pullover. *Gleaner* operated with *May Queen*, both owned by Giles & Hyams, but when they dissolved partnership in the 1920s the two ex-Thames barges were left to rot in the Haven.

North Parade, not far from the Sea View pullover (Sea View Esplanade), when it was only a sand track, around 1910. The dunes, reaching almost up to the parade railings, are now levelled and metalled to form the Sea View municipal car park.

The Young Men's Christian Association provided social clubs for the armed forces all over the country in the First World War (as they did in the Second), and in 1920 the Association used some of its surplus wartime equipment to establish Skegness's first holiday camp, in Grosvenor Road. Walter Hart, from the Nottingham branch, came to take charge and continued as manager until 1953, when he handed over to his son, George. During the winter months, Walter and his staff worked at improving the facilities and gradually the tents and ex-Army huts were replaced by permanent buildings. By 1933 it had become the Woodside Holiday Centre, and the charge for full board for a week was 45s. The 1930s aerial photograph shows how the name, 'Woodside', came to be chosen. At that date, long before Lincoln Road was constructed, the area to the south was mostly grassland. The YMCA closed the centre in 1982 and the site has now been converted to housing, a nursing home and other businesses.

Billy Butlin arrived in Skegness in 1925 with three high-mileaged looking vans crammed with the equipment of a travelling showman. He liked what he saw and decided to put down roots, setting up a small fairground on a patch of the North Parade jungle, about where the County Hotel now stands. There were already amusements on both sides of the parade, but in 1929 the District Council was forced to move all of them to a new site on the south side of the Pier. Butlin was engaged to build the new fairground and given a lease to operate it, which he did right up to 1963. Once this enterprise was running smoothly, he planned his first holiday camp, just inside the Ingoldmells boundary, building by direct labour to the great annoyance of local building contractors. When it opened, at Easter 1936, it was far from finished; the weather was icy, there was no heating, and there were problems with the water supply. The 500 campers had to put up with army camp conditions and struggled to keep warm. Things could only get better, and they did, season by season. New camps were built around the coast, and soon Butlin's became almost as well-known as Woolworth's. During the war the Skegness Butlin's became the Royal Navy recruit training camp, HMS *Royal Arthur*, where thousands of potential sailors trod the concrete decks prior to transferring to ships with water beneath them. Billy Butlin sold out to the Rank Organization in 1972, and in the late '80s the Skegness centre became Funcoast World, though locally it remains Butlin's Camp. Sir William Butlin died in 1980.

On the back of this card, postmarked 11 July 1938, Mildred wrote to her parents in Colne, Lancashire: 'Having a spiffing time, better than last year – biking, putting and rowing. Danced last night with a nice boy from Middlesborough. Playing in a table tennis tournament today. Sunburnt and "in the the pink".' There was always plenty to do or watch at Butlin's, and after all the go-go-go the Viennese Beer Garden would be a good place to take a breather.

Fred Clements brought his first concert party to Skegness in 1900, and in a few years he had become the resort's leading entertainments entrepreneur. Besides his Happy Valley on the sands, he built the Arcadia Theatre and the Tower Cinema and ran other shows at Mablethorpe and Sutton-on-Sea. In the wintertime Clements produced pantomime in a number of inland towns and cities. He died in 1941, aged sixty-six, and is buried in the cemetery at St Clement's.

Drummond Road, with Kimberley House (destroyed by wartime bombing) and, next to it, hidden by a tree, Fred Clements' residence, Arcadia Lodge, which is now Agencia Travel and Cristal Grill. Clements' Arcadia Theatre is in the centre of this 1921 photograph, next-door to his house. The theatre was demolished in 1988 and the site became a council car park in 1992.

Fred Clements at the wheel with his troupers, around 1910.

The Royal Entertainers on stage at Happy Valley, North Parade in the early 1920s.

Clements' Happy Valley concert pitch viewed from North Parade in the 1920s. The paying customers sat on deckchairs and forms and collecting boxes were rattled in front of the free viewers at frequent intervals. The site is now occupied by the Sun Castle.

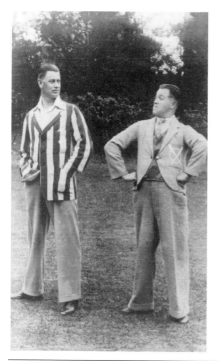

Two popular artistes at Happy Valley at the time were Ted Cartwright (left) and Rob Currie, seen here trousered in the fashionable Oxford Bags of the 1920s.

Burrows & Chilvers' Chalet Theatre stood on the edge of the Jungle, North Parade in the early 1920s, and for several summers presented high-class musical concerts. Before building the Chalet, they had an open-air pitch in the Marine Gardens, Grand Parade, and the evening performances were illuminated by candles in ornamental bowls strung between poles. George Burrows afterwards became Billy Butlin's publicity manager and organized the mammoth street processions and brass band contests held in the mid-1930s. The photograph shows the orchestra seated outside the theatre (now replaced by the Dorchester Hotel) in 1921.

In the low-wage 1920s parents who brought their children on a day trip to the seaside were usually stretching their resources to the limit, and there were no sixpences to spare for seats when a free view of the pierrots could be obtained.

North Parade, Skegness. No. 2829.

North Parade was lined with stalls, skittle alleys, roundabouts, and a variety of other fairground attractions in 1924, with the Figure 8 Switchback at the far end. The first two buildings are photographic studios, George Farmer's far right and Burnham's next to it, and the Chalet Theatre is partly visible on the left.

Looking towards North Parade from the Pier, around 1914, with, left to right, Jimmy Maddox's Pierrots, a parade shelter, Severn's Aerial Flight, Clements' Happy Valley, the Sea View Hotel and the Figure 8 fairground.

Aerial view of the North Parade area in 1929. On the left, the raised cinder path runs from Roman Bank, through some allotments and the Jungle to reach North Parade at Butlin's first amusement park, where 'The Thriller' coaster ride can be seen far right. The newly opened National Deposit Friendly Society's convalescent home (now the Town Hall) is on the left and, beyond it, the Figure 8 Switchback and another large fairground.

The Park, 1910, with the asphalt footpath leading from Scarbrough Avenue to Sea View Road, which is now Park Avenue. Unattended, the Park became overgrown and known as 'the Jungle'. Half of it was taken into the grounds of the convalescent home and the southern half was built upon after Castleton Boulevard opened in 1934. In the 1970s the northern half of the Jungle was cleared for a new police headquarters and blocks of flats were subsequently added.

North Parade, looking south from Butlin's amusement park, about 1928, with scattered sideshows as far as the Chalet Theatre and the rooftop of the Pier Hotel on the skyline. On the sea side, reaching as far as the Pier, are more stalls and the aerial flight.

The view looking north to the Figure 8 Railway and, in the foreground, the footpath from Roman Bank through the Jungle which emerges on North Parade, alongside Butlin's rides and stalls.

An early 1920s photograph of the Jungle pathway which led from the cinder path to reach North Parade in the area of what is now the County Hotel.

The NDFS Memorial Convalescent Home, commemorating the Society's members who died in the First World War, opened in 1927 and became the Town Hall in 1964. The north end of the Jungle (enclosed in the convalescent home grounds) can be seen on this 1950 picture, with Booth's dodgem track and the Figure 8 Switchback on the right.

Butlin's amusement park on North Parade, with mushroom stalls and helter-skelter, in 1928.

Charlie Brewster's Ducking Pond was one of the fairground attractions at North Parade in the 1920s. The fall guy, attired in an early type of wetsuit, sat on a plank and when the wooden ball hit the bullseye a mechanism caused the seat to divide in the middle, giving 'Kelly' a ducking, to the merriment of the spectators.

Jim Lewis's Mini Zoo was another of the attractions on North Parade in the early 1920s, with a bear, baboon, monkeys, parrots, and other 'wonders of the jungle'. The Jungle at the rear of the building would have been a happy habitat for any escapers.

Cartwright's Great Wheel was among the fairground rides on the central beach in 1910. An updated version can still be seen in the modern amusement park.

The Boating Lake in the 1920s, when a motor boat did a lake-length cruise with passengers. Row boats, canoes and the little handle-paddle boats were all available for the more energetic.

A 1927 view of the Boating Lake, disclosing where the first section, which opened in 1924, ended. The lake was extended southward to Princes Parade in 1930. The ornamental fountain, seen in the background, had just been moved to the Fairy Dell from the Marine Gardens to make way for the Embassy and Bathing Pool then under construction.

The Bathing Pool, opened in 1928 as the biggest on the east coast, pictured from the cascade a few summers later. The diving stage and water chutes are off the picture to the right.

The pool's twin water chutes, around 1929, forerunner of the piped chutes which are such an attraction in modern indoor swimming pools. On warm summer days these old fashioned chutes in the open air really were fun.

John Hassall's famous Jolly Fisherman poster with the accompanying slogan first appeared on the billboards in February 1908, advertising the Great Northern Railway's day trips from King's Cross to Skegness for three shillings return. This colour postcard (published by The Photochrom Co. of London), without the rail advertisement, was posted from Skegness to a London address, franked 26 August 1909, the year after the poster was first released. Note how the fisherman's hands are outspread, which is how they were on the first posters. But Hassall's original oil painting, which British Rail presented to Skegness Urban District Council, along with the copyright, in 1965, shows the old salt with wrists bent and fingers drooping slightly downwards. This suggests a last minute change from the artist's painting, although subsequent editions of the poster reverted to the drooping hands version shown on the opposite page.

The Jolly Fisherman poster and slogan have been used to satirize hundreds of different causes and happenings, mostly in a favourable and humorous light. This was the front cover of *Punch*'s special summer number on 18 June 1986. *Punch* proved not quite bracing enough and ceased publication in April 1992.

A summer day in June 1963 captured in this *Grimsby Evening Telegraph* aerial photograph taken at low tide. Now no more the arrow straight Pier dipping into the sea, and only part of the big splash of water which was the open-air Bathing Pool remains. Butlin House, to the left of the Clock Tower, has disappeared, as well as Sandbeck House on the other side, while the Foreshore Centre on the right of Tower Esplanade went in 1972.

SECTION TWO

The Town

Lumley Road in 1910 had no need for yellow lines or pedestrian crossings, and people strolled along the carriageway with never a backward glance. The buildings on the right were still nearly all residences or boarding houses. Hildreds Hotel can be glimpsed on the left, just beyond the public lavatories.

The railway reached Skegness in 1873 when the branch line was extended from Wainfleet, the first train steaming into the new terminus on 28 July that summer. Our 1880 photograph shows the original four platforms, and there were six sidings to accommodate the trip trains on the single line from Firsby Junction.

The Skegness stationmaster with two colleagues, possibly booking clerks, pose for their picture on an apparently deserted station, around 1912. The station was roofed over in 1900, soon after the Great Northern Railway bought out the local company.

Lumley Square in the horse and cart era. On the right is the entrance to the railway station, with landaus waiting for the trains, just as taxis do today. The Lumley Hotel can be seen on the left and, near the entrance to Lumley Road, stands the lifeboat on display, for this photograph was taken on Lifeboat Day, 2 July 1906.

The Long Bar of the Lumley Hotel, opposite the railway station, around 1920. It was demolished in 1987 when the hotel was altered and refurbished.

The Lion Hotel opened in 1881, but the stone lion, sculpted by Richard Winn of Grimsby, had to be brought down to the pavement around 1904 for safety reasons. Frederick (Teddy) Kirkby was landlord when this photograph was taken in 1890.

Barlow's grocery, its appetizing aroma of freshly roasted coffee wafting into Lumley Square, is pictured here in 1902. The popular brand names of Coleman's Mustard, Mazawattee Tea and Cadbury's Cocoa are much in evidence, and whisky was half-a-crown a bottle. James Barlow opened his shop in the early 1890s and he served as a town councillor and was active in other organizations. When the business closed, in the 1920s, the building was taken over by Keightley's, the Boston drapery firm, and remained so for many years.

The Skegness branch of what is now Lloyds Bank began business in the town more than a century ago. In 1881 Garfitt's Bank opened an agency in the Earl of Scarbrough's former estate office on Roman Bank, which became the Town Hall. Ten years later Garfitt's was absorbed by the Capital and Counties Bank and, about 1911, they occupied the Lumley Road premises pictured above. Lloyds took over in 1918. Marshall Bros Grocery, later International Stores, is next door. A building with matching façade stood on the opposite side of Lumley Avenue, and was for many years Frith's Restaurant, as shown below. It was demolished around 1920 when the present Midland Bank was built.

Arthur and Walter Stow came from Sleaford to open their Skegness drapery in Lumley Road in 1895, specializing in low-priced goods on the principle of small profits and quick returns. Their shop stood next to Jefferies' toy arcade, on the south side of the main shopping street, not far from the Lumley Avenue junction. The business closed before the First World War.

'Hot dinners from the joint, with unlimited vegetables, as much as you can eat' cost one shilling at Garratt's Champion Dinner House in the 1890s. James Garratt, with wife and daughter, are pictured here in front of their Lumley Road premises in the area of what is now Hudson's shop and the Shades Hotel.

John Green stands beside his café and confectionery shop at 25 and 27 Lumley Road around 1920. At that date many Lumley Road premises had glass verandahs extending across the pavement, a great boon to shoppers in wet weather. John Green, a member of the Town Council and active in a number of local organizations, was also proprietor of the Pleasure Gardens Pavilion as well as another shop and café in Drummond Road. Near the beginning of the century the Pavilion was used for dances and dinners and was the popular spot for school treats and other outings.

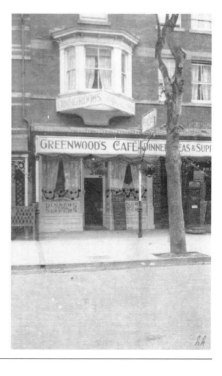

Greenwood's Café at 61 and 63 Lumley Road was a well-known eating house in the earlier years of the century under proprietor Frank Wood and his wife. Cllr Wood, three times chairman of the Urban District Council, established the funeral directors' business which still bears his name. He died in 1944, aged seventy-one. The Café closed when the premises were sold to Marks & Spencer in 1937.

George Morley opened the first Skegness chemist shop in 1874 in a wooden hut in High Street. When Lumley Road was constructed a few years later, he moved to No. 54, in the area where Currys now is. As this 1902 photograph shows, Mr Morley also ran a lending library, but his great speciality was his home-made perfume, 'Skegness Bouquet', sold in a fancy bottle with a label depicting the old parish church.

Bamber's Arcade at 62 Lumley Road in 1902 had an enticing display of postcards, pictures, toys and fancy goods, while horses with handles and children's wooden spades decorated the pavement. Mr Bamber was also a plumber, decorator and 'electrical bell fitter', with a showroom upstairs. The shop is now part of Boots the Chemists.

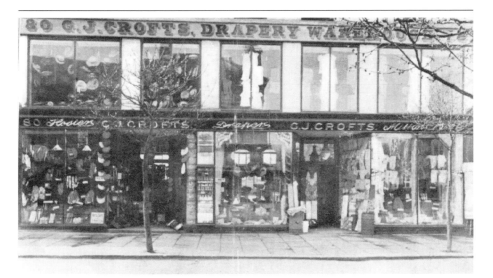

Crofts' drapery stores was for many years the largest shop in Skegness, and there was general regret when it closed in 1983 to be demolished and replaced by Nationwide, Dixons and Baker's Oven. George J. Crofts came to Skegness in 1880 when the new town was under construction, and a 1910 publication eulogized his emporium as a ladies' paradise of millinery of the latest fashion, with hats, including feather boas and other delightful 'feminine falderals'. Mr Crofts was a churchwarden and local councillor and took an active part in many organizations and in particular the annual 'old folks' treat' which ran for many years. He died in 1923.

G.J. Crofts' residence, known as Avondale, on the corner of Algitha Road and Lumley Avenue, pictured in 1904. From the windows he was able to enjoy the view of customers going in and out of his flourishing premises just a few hundred yards away. The building later became the offices of the *Skegness Standard* and it has now been redesigned to accommodate an insurance company.

R.P. Bonnett, at 84 Lumley Road, was established around 1890 as a 'high class pastry-cook, confectioner and bread baker', and continued until near the middle of this century. It is now Wilkinson's meat shop, but the earlier business is commemorated by Bonnett's Restaurant, still in the upstairs rooms.

The Maypole Dairy Co., of 37 Lumley Road, was one of several food multiples in Skegness's main shopping street in the 1930s. Burtons, International and Liptons all had local branches there before self-service supermarkets came into vogue. Maypole's special offers when this photograph was taken included cartons of own-brand teabags, reduced from a shilling to ninepence. The shop is now occupied by Superdrug. Note the unilateral waiting sign on the pavement, when cars were allowed to park on one side of the road on even number days and the opposite side on odd number days. The sign had a hinged half-disc which flipped over to read, 'No Waiting (or Waiting) on this side today'. Early street illuminations, swinging from the treetops, can also be seen.

Chamberlain & Son's café and confectionery shop was in Lumley Road, between the former Dutton's Stores and what is now the Midland Bank, but in the 1930s they moved nearer the Clock Tower, next-door to Blackbourn's shoe shop.

High Street has long been noted for its fish and chips, and Charlie Welsh's establishment stood on the Briar Way corner in the 1920s. A few years later he moved to No. 7, at the Lumley Square end of High Street, where his neighbour at No. 9 sold jellied eels.

A Charles Smyth photograph of Hildreds Hotel after a storm had blown out the eastern bay window and removed tiles in the early 1880s. The hotel was practically rebuilt in 1899 when it was taken over by Bass.

Hildreds Hotel, photographed in March 1987, a month before its demolition to clear the site for the present Hildreds shopping centre.

Oystershell Lane, leading off High Street, in the early 1920s, just after the first Skegness council houses, seen on the right, were completed. The name was changed to Briar Way after it was widened, surfaced and paved. Lord Scarbrough's estate workshops on the left are followed by the taller frontage of Horace Wheatley's shops and lock-up garages. The avenue of garages later became mainly workshops and the bandroom of the Town Band. These gave way to Fred Nicholls' indoor market, and the building was eventually demolished when the ground was cleared for the Hildreds shopping centre. Cllr Wheatley was a long-serving member of the Urban District and County Councils.

Bass Brewery, owners of Hildreds Hotel, erected the Lawn Theatre in 1911 and leased it to Fred Clements who had been running a concert party on the site. In 1921 Clements opened the Tower Theatre and the Lawn was let to Henri DeMond who soon turned it into a picture theatre. Clements also believed that motion pictures were the coming thing, and the Tower was used as a cinema almost from its inception. Our photograph of the Lawn, screening a Pola Negri film, was taken in the 1920 days of silent, black and white pictures. The cast-iron drinking fountain to the right of the public lavatories now stands in front of Natureland, although the aluminium paint has been replaced by gaudier hues. The Tower Theatre (below) is pictured about the same period, next to Smith's Arcade, but it was rebuilt with a new façade after heavy wartime bombing. The Lawn closed early in 1934 (just after the Parade Cinema opened on Grand Parade) and was incorporated, with shops, in Hildreds Hotel.

John Henry Canning, Skegness builder and developer, opened the Central Hall, Roman Bank in 1911, and it was used for public meetings, concerts and dances. Miss Norah Canning held dancing classes there in the 1920s, and when it was converted to the Central Cinema the roof had to be raised several feet. After the cinema closed it was used as a billiards hall, an indoor market and a few other things, but for some years now it has been a bingo hall.

The Casino, North Parade was established in 1922 on the site of an earlier dance hall known as the Alhambra, which had been built in 1911. As well as the ballroom, the Casino specialized in party catering, with seating for 920 at a single sitting. An interesting note in the Casino's brochure on party catering read: 'In common with all other Skegness restaurants, we are not licensed, but if you let us know your requirements *before* the day of your visit we will get in anything you wish.' The majority of much smaller Skegness restaurants have drink licences these days.

Osbert House Hotel around 1920. It became Butlin House in the late 1930s, head office of the by then nationwide leisure company. Butlin's later moved to a new headquarters in London's Oxford Street and the Skegness building was demolished early in 1972.

Osbert House stood at the south end of Frederica Terrace, and here we see the parade elevation of the terrace as it neared completion in 1879. There were no other buildings on Grand Parade at that date and the sands came up to the newly constructed retaining wall. The iron railings in the foreground ran a short distance along what more than forty years later would be Tower Esplanade. Osbert House was named after the ninth Earl of Scarbrough's youngest brother, the Hon. Osbert Lumley.

The north end of Frederica Terrace around 1920, with the Callow Park Hotel added. It is now the Jolly Fisherman and the section on the left the Parade Hotel. The forecourts of Frederica Terrace were built out to the public pavement in 1992.

The ornate Sandbeck Residential Hotel in 1920, the first building on South Parade, was kept by Mr and Mrs T.W. Skinner, who also had butcher shops in the town. The Sandbeck was pulled down in 1972 to be replaced by shops and cafes. The name Sandbeck, prominent in Skegness, is taken from the Earl of Scarbrough's residence, Sandbeck House and Park, near Maltby, South Yorkshire.

The east end of Lumley Road about 1880, with Lumley Terrace (right) and Gomersall Terrace just completed. The roadway is still in a rough state. Harrington Gardens was afterwards built between the two terraces to form a continuous block. Fifty years later the boarding houses and residences began building out over the front gardens to form shops. Across the road (below) was the tree-bordered entrance to the Pleasure Gardens, with the Reading Room (now the National Westminster Bank) in the top right-hand corner of the picture. Hildreds Hotel can be seen in the centre, where High Street joins Lumley Road.

The three Lumley Road terraces photographed in the late 1920s, shortly before shops began to roll out across the front gardens.

Harrington Boarding House, near the centre of the block, was typical of many in this row. In the 1920s the Harrington was kept by Mrs Bernard.

Skegness Steam Laundry Co., Roman Bank was established in 1877 and is pictured here in 1910. The Fry family took it over in 1923 and it was progressively enlarged to become Fenland Laundries, with operations in several other towns. The Roman Bank laundry was devastated by fire in 1975 and the familiar Victorian façade was replaced in almost a complete rebuilding.

The Hygienic Sanitary Laundry Co. opened on what was then Wainfleet Road in 1907 with a Mr J. Hunter as managing director. When the business closed in the 1930s, Wainfleet Road had been realigned, leaving the building on Old Wainfleet Road, in the vicinity of Grandways supermarket. The similarity in layout of the two laundries is very noticeable, and even the delivery vans look much the same.

The Derbyshire Poor Children's Seaside Home was founded by H.B. Sykes (1868—1941) of Derby in the 1890s. The first summer he brought parties of children from poor Derby homes for a week's holiday in rented accommodation in the High Street building (left), which is now part of Crofts Homecare. A few years later he had raised enough money to build the present handsome home in Scarbrough Avenue, pictured above, about 1900. For many years after the Second World War the home was looked after by Jim Stuart BEM and his wife. Jim, a keen amateur photographer, died in 1991, aged 66.

H. Stow & Son's Roman Bank butchery, opposite the post office, closed down in 1988 after trading in the same premises for most of the century. This was their Christmas display around 1936.

Stow's Outfitters, Roman Bank between Harry Stow's butcher shop and H.B. Smith, tobacconist, photographed in 1928. It belonged to Walter Stow, Harry's brother, who had had a similar business in Lumley Road. Walter Stow's daughter, Marion, stands in the doorway. It was absorbed in the butchery premises around 1932.

Randall's fish and fruit shop, Roman Bank around 1908, with Mr and Mrs Randall and their daughter and three employees. On the far right is John Henry Canning who built most of the pre-1914 houses in Grosvenor Road, Dorothy Avenue and Cecil Avenue. He was also the first person in Skegness to have his own electric lighting, in 1904, the dynamo being worked by a gas engine.

Walter Cook established his butchery business on Roman Bank before the First World War, but he moved into Randall's former shop (above) soon after the war ended. His new shop front, seen here in 1928, remains much the same today. Left to right: Fred Fletcher, Bert Platt, Syd Ranson, Bert Gray and John Mitchell, with schoolboys Hedley and Walter (Bib) Cook in front.

Scarbrough Avenue and the Pier slice through this 1938 aerial photograph, and to the left can be seen the backs of the private hotels on North Parade. In the left foreground, on the corner of Park Avenue, is the Red House Hotel, destroyed in October 1942 in the town's most destructive air raid, when twelve people died, sixty-one were injured and eleven houses were wiped off the map.

The fronts of the North Parade hotels, including the County (right), can be seen in this photograph taken around the same period, with the Sun Castle and bowling greens prominent and the curving Waterway in the bottom left corner.

Scarbrough Avenue was still a gravel road, with no kerb or gutter, in the 1920s when this picture was taken. The milk float carries two churns at the back from which the milkman filled his pail. Driving down the middle of the road seemed to present no hazards.

The view to the right of the milk float in 1926, with the imposing Parkside on the right. It was built around 1880 for the Hudsons, a family who produced three generations of talented musicians. In 1926 Parkside was part of the Orient Girls' College, which had an excellent reputation, under Mr and Mrs Boyer. The college took in the adjacent Leeson Lodge, College House (now New Park Club) and Harewood (now Charnwood Hotel). Some years later Parkside became the Red House Hotel with a large west wing, but was destroyed by bombs in 1942. It remained a ruin for several decades before the present residential flats were built on the site. Leeson Lodge became the residence of Cllr Frank Wood.

The sea-water swimming baths in Scarbrough Avenue began business in 1882, with separate pools for ladies and gents, private baths and Turkish baths. The water supply was through a gravity pipeline from the sea, boosted by a suction pump. When mixed bathing became permissible at the beginning of the century, the ladies' pool (below) was boarded over to become the King's Theatre and the men's section was opened to both sexes. The Turkish baths had already fallen into disuse when Elijah Parker took over the baths in the 1920s and as they were partly heated, advertised them as Skegness Tepid Seawater Baths. The whole building was wiped out by enemy bombs in the Second World War and the site was afterwards cleared for the present council car park.

The old haven town of Skegness was washed into the sea in 1526 and it is recorded that for some years afterwards the church spire could be seen at low tide. When the town was rebuilt, a new church, well out of reach of the waves, was dedicated to St Clement who was martyred at sea. Stones reclaimed from the old church were used to help build the new, which, utilitarian rather than beautiful, was the work of poor people whose possessions had been stolen by the tide. St Clement's in the fields (below) served the small community for several centuries until the resort town was planned with a much larger and more central church. The new St Matthew's (above) in Scarbrough Avenue was designed by James Fowler of Louth. The Countess of Scarbrough laid the foundation stone on 5 November 1879 and the partly completed building was consecrated by Christopher Wordsworth, Bishop of Lincoln, on 21 September the following year. The two churches are pictured around 1905.

Rutland Terrace, Rutland Road was built in the early 1880s, costing altogether £4,400. In the slump which began around 1883 builder T.L. Kassell, unable to sell many of the houses, was forced into bankruptcy. The north end of the terrace, photographed in the 1890s, opened in 1882 as the Revd E.R. Iremonger's boarding school 'for the young sons of gentlemen'. It later became the Essendon School for Girls, but in the Second World War, known as Pembroke House (the name of the former boys' school), it was the local Civil Defence headquarters. It has for some years now been the Masonic Hall.

St Winifred's Girls' School and Prep School for Boys, under principal Miss Broad, pictured in 1910, was near the middle of Rutland Terrace. Also in the terrace was the Ilkeston Convalescent Home.

The Vine Hotel opened around 1770 as the Skegness Inn, but some time after Thomas Enderby took over in 1828 it was renamed Enderby's Hotel and only became known as the Vine much later in the century.

Coronation Walk was laid out to commemorate the crowning of Edward VII in 1901 and this photograph was taken soon afterwards, when the trees and shrubs were quite small. Coronation Walk, starting in Drummond Road, links up with Vine Walk at the Vine Hotel (seen in the background) and runs on to Richmond Drive.

Drummond Road in 1905 was little more than a mud track in winter, but it was made up a few years later as traffic to the Seacroft golf links, as well as new houses, increased. Compare it with the picture opposite; Crey's grocery (later Brown's) can be seen at the junction with Clifton Grove in both. In the early 1900s most of the avenues on the sea side of Drummond Road were just sand tracks leading up to the dunes.

Green's Drummond Road garage when Morris Minors were selling like hot cakes. It had opened as W.O. Knott's Garage, the largest in Skegness, just after the First World War, but it is now a wholesale food warehouse.

Children playing on Drummond Road in the almost traffic-free 1920s. The garage sign is pointing down Clifton Grove to the Seacroft Garage, and Brown's grocery and post office stands at the junction. George Frederick Ball's domed advertising stand can be seen on the wide pavement farther along on the right. The auctioneer and estate agent was advertising holiday bungalows to let and, among other things, the sale of 300 pairs of lace curtains, bedroom suites, pianos, a baker's cart and a tub cart. With this octagonal advertising stand, one might claim that Mr Ball anticipated the modern street billboard cylinder by about sixty years. The Pavilion auction rooms were in the Tower Gardens.

Roman Bank at the junction with Algitha Road, with the Council Offices (later Town Hall) centre and post office on the right, around 1920. The Council Offices had been built as the Earl of Scarbrough's estate offices. The post office moved to a new building across the road in 1929 and their old premises are now the Trustees Savings Bank.

Dexter's Stores, Roman Bank (near the Sea View Road junction) in the first half of this century sold everything from bags of sugar and biscuits to wines and spirits and ladies' and children's clothing. Mrs Dexter is pictured, around 1914, with her children, Doris and Horace, standing in the doorway of their house next to the shop.

Aerial view of Roman Bank, Winthorpe in the early 1920s, with the Royal Oak Hotel standing in open fields and a solitary motor bus making its way towards the town. Winthorpe Avenue branches off to the right, but in the far distance, where Billy Butlin was to build his holiday camp, are more fields. Royal Oak Terrace (below), just north of the hotel, faces another patch of grassland, with the Nottinghamshire Miners' Convalescent Home (later Seely House) visible on the right. The convalescent home was demolished in 1980.

The Ship Hotel dated from the 1830s and was demolished in 1936, after a new Ship had been erected in Castleton Boulevard, just across the road. The 'bluestone' boulder, standing beneath the window to the right of the stepped entrance, was a relic of the detritus washed down from Scotland after the last Ice Age. It remained in front of the Ship for many years and is now lodged at the Church Farm Museum.

Burgh Road Bridge, with wooden handrails, pictured here in 1907, carried the main road traffic from Lincoln across the Winthorpe Drain. The bridge was replaced when the A158 was widened in the 1920s, but the drain running from the cemetery was not piped and filled until many years later. Part of Ivy House can be seen on the right of the picture.

Erected in 1927, the reinforced concrete water tower at the Burgh Road Waterworks is seen alongside the much earlier brick tower. When the storage tank of the new tower was filled with water the building lurched alarmingly and had to be hastily emptied. Extra piling eventually stabilized it, although it remained several feet out of plumb. Skegness's answer to the more famous tower in Pisa was demolished in 1981. During the 1950s Skegness was almost beyond the range of the television transmitter and the BBC placed a booster on top of the water tower until the erection of the Belmont TV mast made it unnecessary.

The beam wireless station at Winthorpe began operating in 1927, receiving messages from India and Australia, with a transmitting station at Tetney, near Grimsby. The Skegness installation, in Church Lane West, comprised eight steel masts, some 300 ft tall, five serving India and three Australia. They were dismantled in 1940 because of danger to aeroplanes and moved to Somerset.

Coastguard Cottages, St Andrews Drive are listed in the 1851 census (but not in 1841) with five officers and their families at Nos 1 to 5 Maitland Place. It may have been named after Major-General Maitland who had commanded the county regiment earlier in the century. The coastguard station, still called The Lookout, stands a few yards away on top of the dune, but it and the five cottages are now privately occupied. An additional coastguard station was established at Gibraltar Point a few years later, also manned by five officers.

When Gibraltar Point Coastguard Station was built in 1859 it was close to the river and seashore but the sea has receded, leaving it some distance from the water. The coastguards operated here until about 1922 but the building is now incorporated in the Nature Trust study centre.

SECTION THREE

The People

Gas street lighting needed regular checking and cleaning, and Charlie North is here servicing a lamp in Wainfleet Road. The transition to electricity was not completed until the 1950s.

Skegness railway station workers, 1922. Standing far right is taxi driver Freddy Vickers, whose family gave the name to Vickers Point, Ingoldmells. Freddy was often known as the Baron de Boeuf, after a popular mustard advertisement of that period. The bearded gentleman seated at the other end of the front row is A.G. Martin, manager of the W.H. Smith bookstall. The photograph was taken in front of the goods office and the regular station bobby has a front row seat.

The 1906 railway staff ran to about two dozen when most of the traffic in and out of Skegness was by train.

Skegness's Merryweather horse-drawn fire-engine, purchased in 1913, with Vin Sandaver in the driving seat and engineer Charlie Houlden behind.

Skegness Volunteer Fire Brigade posed with their solid-tyred Dennis outside the Imperial Café around 1934. Back row standing, left to right: Steve Rogers, Colin Jones, Art Sewell, Frank Burbidge, Alec Bell. Seated, centre: Ted Epton, George Kemp, H. Shaw and driver George Strickland. Front: Cyril Kay, J. Topliss, Hugh Eagle, Fred Smith, Jack Leeman, Jack Bell and chief officer Joe Davy.

The 'likely lads' of Skegness 1920 pose a moment as they enjoy their Sunday afternoon stroll along Grand Parade, or perhaps they are just watching the girls go by. Left to right are Harry Wood, Bill Bellamy, Lance Grunnill, George Wood, -?-, -?-, Archie Osbourne, George Thompson, Aubrey Green and Ezra Keyworth. All with collars, ties and headgear and, no doubt, shiny shoes.

Skegness St John Ambulance Brigade around 1920. Standing, left to right: W. Clayworth, -?-, -?-, Cyril Shepherd, Jim Chadwick, -?-, J.R. Shepherd, A.G. Martin, -?-, Bob Hovell, -?-, H. Land. Seated: -?-, -?-, George Dunkley, Tom Smith and Sid Sellars.

The Royal Antediluvian Order of Buffaloes established their headquarters in Briar Way in the early 1920s and the building afterwards became the present Skegness Working Men's Club. In this 1940s photograph Ted Epton occupies the seat of honour, surrounded by other members of the Charles Farmer Lodge in full regalia.

The Skegness Chicks, a product of the dancing school of Mrs Lily Crane (née Langham), were a popular turn at many local concerts and they are pictured here around 1930, with 'beaks' turned aside to show their faces. Back row, left to right: Florrie Hydes, -?-, -?-, Violet Girling, Lorraine Atkin, -?-, M. Gray. Second row: Peggy Burrell, Zilla Good, Bessie Lakin, Bessie Warren, Cecily Brown, Freda Sutton, Norah Tarr, Barbara Dingley. Third row: Doris Bell, -?-, Helen Draper, Phyllis Hydes, -?-, Irene Hydes, -?-, Peggy Stevenson, Edna Parkins. Front: -?-, Gwen Clifford, Billy Clayworth.

Ridging potatoes around 1920, with Darby (left) and Duke, piloted by Henry Wilkinson who was born at the nearby Marsh Farm, Richmond Drive. Henry was later to become well known in Skegness as an amateur actor and a professional photographer.

John Burn, far left, of Church Farm (now Church Farm Museum) with landworkers employed on the farms of W.J. Cook & Sons in 1929. Next to Mr Burn are, left to right: Jack Good, Vic Burn, Jimmy Sharp, George Stones and Frank Maddison. On the ground, left to right, the last three girls are believed to be Violet, Daisy and Jean Maddison.

Fred Rowe ran the livery stables adjoining Hildreds Hotel, and in this 1905 photograph his smart coaches are displayed to prospective hirers.

Hildreds Hotel, like the other larger Skegness hotels, sent a private coach to meet the trains and collect patrons and their luggage, a service which lasted well into the 1920s.

John Borman began business in Skegness about 1880, carrying goods with the aid of a
borrowed donkey. Eventually he was able to buy a pony, and by the turn of the century
he was employing half a dozen horses and nine men in his haulage and coal business. John
Borman's son and grandson continued the trade and John Borman I is standing in the
centre of this photograph.

John Hydes contracted with the LNER to deliver goods arriving at the station and this is
one of his drays proceeding along Grand Parade, with the Callow Park Hotel (now Jolly
Fisherman) on the left.

In the 1930s the Urban District Council's transport was only partly motorized and horses and carts carried out most of the work on the roads. Bill Sellars is here driving one of their fine nags along South Parade. The Council's last two horses, Captain and Brandy, were not retired until 1957, when carts, harness and all equipment were sold by auction. The two horses went to a farm at Tetford.

Horses needed regular shoeing, and there were three Skegness black-smiths, two at Roman Bank and one in Prince George Street. Bill Neale's smithy was at 57 Roman Bank and he worked it for thirty years, until his death in 1962. By then, there were few working horses left, but he had been helped by Truelove's riding stables at the Old Hall, which employed quite a large number of horses. Bill Neale's blacksmith shop was near the present John Wilson Furnishers.

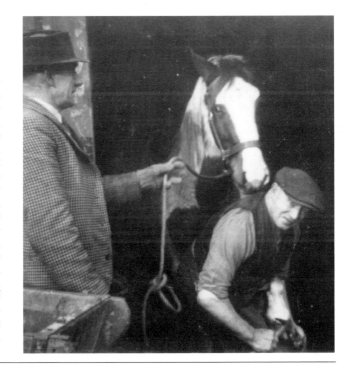

John Green's bakery van in 1905, when bread as well as milk was delivered to the door.

Jack Parkins trots his horse along North Parade, drawing a milk float belonging to the Skegness Farmers' Dairy Co., in the pre-bottle, bucket and jug days of the 1930s.

Up until the 1920s the pillar-box red royal mailcart took letters and parcels from Skegness post office to catch the mail train at Burgh Station, six miles away, bringing back the incoming post. Driver Frank Turner stands ready with his galloper before setting off across the marsh.

Postman Green pedals a parcel tricycle, with wicker container, along Grand Parade around 1930.

Charles Hannam came to Skegness from Lincoln in the 1920s and built Triumph House on Roman Bank to sell pianos and other musical instruments. He had similar businesses in Lincoln and Gainsborough and was reputed to be the second man in Lincoln, after R.M. Wright, to own a motor car. Here, he is taking his wife for a spin, around 1905. The Skegness shop later turned to radio and television, in charge of Clifford Hannam, and is now Yates & Greenhough.

In the days when you had to swing a handle to start your car, with George Wood's saloon standing in Algitha Road, his son, young Tony, got in some early practice. The house on the left, next to the Methodist church, was destroyed by bombs during the Second World War and was never rebuilt.

In the 1920s and '30s there were several one-vehicle haulage contractors with either a horse and cart or lorry, and this is J.K. Frost's outfit shifting sand.

Skegness had three mineral water firms in the years between the wars: Bellamy Bros in Alexandra Road, Askey's in Church Road, and Apollo on Roman Bank. Bellamys' solid-tyred Napier is seen here loaded with crates outside the bottling factory and, left to right, ? Hickson, ? Green and Bill Poucher.

A launch of the *Samuel Lewis* in the early 1920s, with men and horses preparing to drag the carriage away from the lifeboat. In the lower picture the oarsmen are pulling away under the command of coxswain Matthew Grunnill.

The lifeboat was hauled by eight Shire horses, kept on a local farm, until the first caterpillar tractor was allocated to the Skegness station in 1926, saving much time and energy in the launching operation. During a practice, in February 1936, the tractor broke down and this is a picture of the team of horses recruited to bring the *Anne Allan* across the beach at low tide. That first lifeboat tractor had seen service in the First World War hauling guns, so it was by no means a new machine when it reached Skegness.

Tom Darcy driving the first tractor, in attendance on the *Anne Allan*, Skegness's first motor lifeboat, which was in service 1932–53. Wilf Grunnill is standing in front of the tractor.

George Perrin was born in a house-boat (*Noah's Ark*) at Gibraltar Point, where his father was a fisherman. He served in smacks and deep sea trawlers out of Grimsby, eventually as mate, but returned to Skegness to take over his father's fishing boat when he died. George Perrin joined the lifeboat crew in 1912 and succeeded Matthew Grunnill as coxswain in 1932, taking charge of the first Skegness motor lifeboat, *Anne Allen*. He was away on minesweeping trawlers in the First World War, and in the Second he took the Skegness lifeboat to the rescue of many crashed planes, friend and foe alike. George Perrin retired in 1947 and died five years later, aged 74.

Wilfred (Bill) Perrin, George's son, was brought up at Gibraltar Point, when the family lived in the former Ship Inn, and he became lifeboat coxswain on his father's retirement. Bill Perrin had grown up in small boats and was a crewman in the Skegness lifeboat from 1921, when he was only seventeen. He saw the transition from sail and oars to motor lifeboats and was second coxswain under his father from 1934 before serving another sixteen years as coxswain, from 1947 until 1963. F.S.W. Major, in his *Skegness Lifeboats*, rated Bill Perrin 'one of the finest fore and aft seamen on the East Coast'.

Matthew Grunnill was coxswain of the Skegness lifeboat from 1908 to 1932 and he was awarded a silver medal by the King of Norway for the lifeboat's brave rescue of the eight man crew of the Norwegian brig *Azha* in 1912. He spent sixty years as a lifeboatman and we see him here in retirement turning his hand to collecting funds for the RNLI with some assistance from his four-footed friend. Matt Grunnill died in 1940.

Cockle boat off Skegness manned by, left to right, Alf, Mont and Gip Gunnill, *c.* 1900.

Proud parents Mr and Mrs Bert Holland in front of their Roman Bank home, with auntie holding the baby. The lusty infant was to become an even sturdier adult and eventually coxswain of the Skegness lifeboat, 1965–85. Ken Holland BEM has also served as town mayor and is the chairman of East Lindsey District Council for the second time.

Sailing ships were sometimes beached at Skegness for breaking up, and this early 1900s photograph shows a dismantling gang with horse and cart ready to lead away the timbers. It could have been the *Eliza* museum ship, which was auctioned and sold as wreckage in 1912.

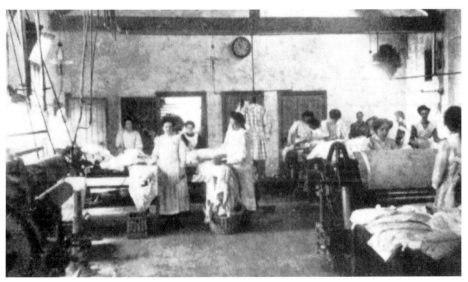

A workroom at Skegness Steam Laundry, Roman Bank around 1920.

Snaps Corner, at the junction of High Street and Lumley Road, where, in the early 1920s, Mr Snaps, alias Bert Jackson, first displayed 'walking snapshots'. It was also a booking office for Clements' entertainments, where Mr Snaps had the exclusive right to take photographs of the audience. Mrs Jackson can be seen behind the counter and comedian Jimmy Loft makes a personal appearance to boost his benefit night. The other side of the block, now Tonglet's, was known as Turner's Corner because of the restaurant of that name.

'Big Ernie' Woods' newspaper barrow, in the summers up to the early 1930s, was looked upon as almost an extension of the Clock Tower. Ernie was an astute salesman and, in the winter months, as soon as the local papers came out he would scan the wedding reports and photographs and, with a bagful over his shoulder, nip round to the homes of all the happy couples' parents, greeting each one with, 'There's a lovely picture of your son/daughter in the paper today, missus. How many would you like?' Big Ernie usually unloaded at least half a dozen copies at each stop. He died in 1934.

Grosvenor Road being surfaced around 1910, when there were very few buildings beyond what was then the Nottingham Women's Convalescent Home, seen in the centre. In those days roadmaking needed a large work-force using forks, shovels and barrows.

In contrast, half a century later, when Lincoln Road was constructed heavy machinery was employed, with much less labour. Lincoln Road opened in 1960 to provide a direct route from Burgh Road (A158) to the town centre. Council road ganger Johnny Foreman stands near the spreader facing the camera.

Skegness Town Band around 1912. Disbanded at the outbreak of war a couple of years later, the band was not revived until 1928.

Skegness Excelsior Band was formed in 1935 when most of the Salvation Army Band, including the bandmaster, resigned over the right to visit the cinema, a diversion strictly against Army regulations. Bandmaster Petch is shown here with his new band, flanked by two of their supporters, Cllr Frank Evans (left) and Jack Hardacre, who had a music shop in Lumley Road. The band enjoyed considerable success but did not reform after the war.

The 1st Skegness Company, Boys' Brigade, with OC Captain R.H. Jenkins behind the big drum and, on his right, Revd H.W. Hunt and Lieut George Lillyman and, on his left, Lieut Wilfred Keyworth. This photograph was taken outside the Baptist church, possibly in the late 1940s.

The 1st Skegness Group of Boy Scouts in the Tower Gardens, 1926, with Scoutmaster Bernard Northern, centre, and Assistant Scoutmaster Spence on his right.

Fred Stamper was a regular in Skegness carnival processions for many years, either in the guise of Gandhi or the Skegness Jolly Fisherman, the latter necessitating a pillow packing operation. Fred autographed this photograph: 'Darkly yours, F.W. Stamper, "Skegness Gandhi", 1931–2.'

Alfred Haywood opened his Skegness rock factory in Rose Grove in 1920, later moving to a new building in Cavendish Road. He is seen here (extreme right) with his carnival entry in the early '20s. The girls are in working overalls. A stick of Skegness rock, with the name printed all the way through, became an almost obligatory gift to take home after a visit to the seaside. Haywood's rock factory closed down in 1962.

What was this group doing, photographed (on a glass plate) at Sundial Farm off Warth Lane around 1870? The backboard reads 'Fanny', and they appear to be staging an open-air play. The ancient Sundial Farm was occupied in this century by the Hipkins and then the Mowbrays and was demolished in 1960 to make way for the Council's Sundial Housing Estate.

Fireman Arthur Sewell has a pair of his donkeys yoked to the old fire-engine in this late 1940s carnival procession. Alongside is one of the UDC's small-wheeled S&D refuse collecting freighters, with driver Arthur Hill beside it, wearing the cap. Charles Lane's furniture van is in the right background.

Woolworth's Lumley Road staff in 1938, before checkouts replaced counter service. It was a 'nothing over 6d' stores in those days, but it is surprising what you could buy for a tanner. The Skegness branch had opened in 1928.

Rolling out the barrels at The Shades, Lumley Road, in the early 1920s, with landlord Fred Selby chatting to the railway deliveryman.

Jack Marshall (left) and John Nelson formed a popular comedy duo at many local functions in the 1920s and '30s and both were prominent members of Skegness Amateur Dramatic Society. Marshall & Son were Lumley Road jewellers and John Nelson came to Skegness to work for them before setting up his own business in Drummond Road.

Cyril Cowpe and his Band pictured in the Embassy Ballroom in the early 1950s. This was one of the town's most popular dance bands from the 1930s right through to the 1950s. Left to right: Harold Buttery, Jack Green, Ian Taylor, Peggy Boosey, Cyril Cowpe and Frank Terrington.

A.E. Fletcher was the first editor of the *Skegness Standard* when it was launched by the Lincolnshire Standard group in July 1922. He was editor, reporter and advertising manager, working alone in his own house until the new paper got on its feet. Offices were eventually taken in Algitha Road, with Ernest Kelly attending to the advertisements, and its circulation quickly increased. During his thirty years' editorship, Arthur Fletcher contributed a weekly commentary under the *nom de plume* of 'The Old Salt', a football report by 'Touchline' and, periodically, a humorous dialect tale by 'Hayeeheff'. He served with distinction on the urban council and died suddenly in 1952 while still editing the paper he had created.

The *Skegness News* was inaugurated by Charles Henry Major in 1909 and, six years afterwards, he acquired John Avery's old-established *Skegness Herald*, and eventually absorbed it in the *News*. His son, F.S.W. Major (right), held the editorial reins for many years until ill health forced his retirement and the *News* closed down in 1964. Always interested in the sea, Stanley Major served on minesweepers during the Second World War, finishing with the rank of lieutenant-commander He wrote several commemorative booklets on different aspects of Skegness history, particularly the lifeboat, with which he was connected for more than fifty years, and he was chairman of the Skegness branch of the RNLI when he died in 1974. The *Skegness News* was revived by Mortons of Horncastle in 1985.

Canon Arthur Henry Morris was rector of Skegness, 1929–37, after occupying vicarages at Crowland and Gainsborough. During his incumbency he restored the former parish church of St Clement, which was almost derelict, and brought it back into useful service. 'The canon', as he was usually referred to, was a much loved minister and took an active part in the affairs of the town, and particularly in the local lifeboat. He moved to Denton, near Grantham, but returned to spend his retirement in Skegness where he took up his earlier interests until his death in 1965 at the age of 92. The former Morris Secondary School, Morris Gardens and Morris Walk were all named after him.

The Skegness Window Cleaning Company was in business in the 1920s and the young joint managing directors were Edwin Lewis (left) and his brother-in-law, Len Fisher, pictured here with their equipage.

Sunday Schools enjoyed their greatest popularity in the decade following the First World War, when the 'anniversary' and 'school treat' were much anticipated events in the juvenile calendar. Here we see the Baptist Sunday School, with superintendent R.H. Jenkins left of centre, grouped outside their church in 1924.

Skegness Primitive Methodists grouped in front of Ivy House, Wainfleet Road around 1912. John O. Smith, a prominent member of the church, farmed at Ivy House and the gathering has assembled for a celebration of some kind. 'J.O.' later moved to Dean's Farm, nearer town.

'The Prims' pose ready for a picnic on the sandhills, round about the same date. Samuel Moody is on the far left and next to him is John Banham, both leading Methodists.

A class of fifty-nine nine- and ten-year-olds at the former Skegness National School, Roman Bank, photographed in Ida Road in 1923. Back row, left to right: Frances Coulson, L. Howard, Amy Kime, Doris Lill, Mary Henstridge, R. Elliot, G. Hardy, A. Wilson, Eva Girling, Muriel McClatchey, Winnie Booth, D. Severn, Doreen Armstrong, M. Hill, Mary Wright, M. Horwell, Phyllis Hardy, Olive Bell, M. Wilson, Norah Watson. Second row: Nancy Jenner, Walter Girling, ? Atkin, Wilfred Pullon, George Cumberworth, -?-, D. Slack, Ivy Sharman, G. Topley, ? Mimmack, ? Wright, A. North, ? Panter, Gilbert Mastin, -?-, -?-. Third row: Ernest Moult, Philip Halliday, Gordon Bradley, O. Green, Jack Leeman, ? Ellis, Donald Goodacre, Olaf Lunn, Leslie Allenby, ? Gollings, -?-, ? Ashenden. Front row, on ground: John Osbourne, Hedley Cook, Bill Saint, Reg Eldred, George Hunter, John Miller, ? Pountney, Frank Moody, -?-, Percy Woodward, Edgar Whiting.

Skegness Grammar School sixth form, 1962. Back row, left to right: Paul Dorling, John Clark, Trevor Purnell, Alan Faux, Graham Baggaley, D.A. Penton, ? Garner. Middle row: Elizabeth Pearson, Elizabeth Barnes, Angela Manning, Patricia Fanthorpe, Stephanie Wise, Irene Spence, Marian Badley, Patricia Kime, Gillian Poyser. Front row: Jennifer Murray, Susan Burrell, Jean Mowbray, Pat Youngfir, Ann Davies, R.A. Hall, Anthony Hall, Don Brereton, Michael Waugh, Garth Fisher.

A Skegness hockey team, near the beginning of the century, posed on a pitch at Seacroft. Names are unknown except for the left hand player standing, who is believed to be a Dutton.

Orient Girls' College hockey team, Skegness 1923. Standing, left to right: Alice Moore, Mary Wheatley, Marjorie Needham, Gertrude Huggins and the games mistress. Seated: Katherine Eastwood, Mollie Geraty, Kathleen Moore, Joan Hammerton, -?-, Vernie Stocks and Connie Savage.

Skegness Urban District Council, 1922–3. Back row, left to right: H. Mather (treasurer), W. Clifford (gasworks manager), William Frearson (part time town clerk), V.H. Tippet (assistant town clerk), R.H. Jenkins (engineer, surveyor and sanitary inspector). Middle row: two unknown councillors, C.T. Jessap, Thomas Marshall, Hedley Thornton, Walter Hudson, John W. Borman, Frank Wood, H. Vasey (waterworks manager). Front: Councillors W. Plasket Moody, Dr B. Sweeten, David C. Haley, Samuel Moody (chairman), Charles Bycroft, G. Goodess and George F. Ball. Politics had not intruded into Skegness local government in the 1920s and all fifteen members sat as Independents.

Skegness Urban District Council, 1953–4. Standing, left to right: H.M. Cooper (deputy engineer and surveyor), L.J. Parker (catering manager), Sydney James (health inspector), Milton Turner (deputy town clerk), D.T. Edwards (engineer and surveyor), Ivor M. Cule (town clerk), T.E. Hirst (treasurer), H. Mather (deputy treasurer), Dr Fraser Menzies (medical officer of health), W.G. Bosworth (foreshore director), Percy Shaw (assistant foreshore director). Middle row: Councillors Louis J. Walthall, George E. Swaby, Alfred Denham, Mrs Elsa Barratt (chairman), Joseph Crawshaw, Reginald J.G. Dutton, Arthur Corden, Albert E. Thompson. Front: Councillors J.H. Edwards, Eric Watson, Cyril Catlyn, T.S. Bellamy, Harold Bayes, Walter Hart, John D. Williamson. John Hassall's original 'Jolly Fisherman' painting hangs on the wall of the Roman Bank Council Chamber.

The destruction of the Pier in 1978 was a particularly sad occasion for Skegness Pier Angling Club whose activities have since been largely restricted to fishing from the beach or from a boat. A festival competition from the pierhead (above) in 1961, with current club president, John Collier, nearest the camera and former secretary, Colin Hill, next to him. Below: three club members in the 1930s, well protected from the sea breeze, derive a lot of amusement from a not very impressive catch.

Pigeon racing has been the chosen sport for a select band of Skegness enthusiasts for most of the century, and none has been more successful than Charlie North, winner of numerous trophies, seen here at his loft in the late 1940s.

Skegness Wheelers Cycling Club was formed early in 1933, successor to a similar organization which flourished for a year or two in the 1890s. The Wheelers were, at one time, the second largest club in Lincolnshire after Scunthorpe Polytechnic. Pictured, left to right, are: Terry Hayter, Johnny Storey, Dennis Probert, Walter Girling and Frank Bridle after winning the team prize in Louth Wheelers' Open 50 Miles time trial around 1950.

An overnight stop in the 1930s at Ruckland Youth Hostel in the Wolds, when accommodation cost a shilling a night with breakfast for a few extra coppers. Hostellers had to carry out a few chores before departure and the Wheelers, prepared for a spot of lawn-mowing and woodchopping, are, back row, left to right: Sam Stubbins, Billy Bell, Winston Kime, Esme Crow, John Robinson and two other hostellers. Front: Mollie Chandler, Elsie Thompson, Bertha Thompson and Frank Bridle.

This 1912 photograph of the town bowling green shows the Old Hall, Roman Bank in the background, and, from left to right, the first three bowlers are Tom Greenwood, George Randall and Ralph Hudson. The former Town Hall can be glimpsed on the right. Sutton Court now takes up part of this area.

A tennis tournament on the Richmond Drive cricket ground in 1908. Surrounded by great trees, the ground lost much of its beauty in 1981, when the trees had to be felled because of the Dutch elm epidemic.

Around 1950 George Edward Ball got together this team of veterans, with a mixture of youth, to face another scratch eleven on the Richmond Drive cricket ground. Pictured outside the pavilion, standing left to right, are: umpire Batty, Derrick Barker, Gordon Wright, Tony Wood, Stan Watson, Brian Dexter, Herrick Watson. Seated: Herbert Simpson, J. Nicholson, Bill Maddison, George Ball, Jack Tinn and Albert Starr.

A Nottinghamshire County XI played Skegness & District at Richmond Drive in September 1931, the visitors including England players Harold Larwood, Bill Voce, Sam Staples and George Gunn. Notts. scored 210 for 6 declared and Skegness replied with 138 for 3 to draw the match. Raymond Frearson, Skegness and Lincolnshire's top batsman, contributed 100 not out. Larwood, who took two of the Skegness wickets, is seated far right.

Skegness & District FC photographed after defeating Alford 1–0 in the final of the Willoughby Cup, played at Spilsby on 28 April 1901. Committee members standing at the back are: J. Barlow, R. Turner, W. Enderby, F.B. Storr, C. Hemm, F. Kirkby and G. Greenwood, while the players are: S. Buxton, H. Manton and C. Falkinder; H. Charlton, W.M. Epton (capt.) and J. Hanson; S. Hewson, J. Heaton, R.H. Huggins, A. Burchnall and G. Burley. A few seasons later the club became Skegness United, playing in an all-white strip as 'the Lilywhites', a tradition continued since 1946 by Skegness Town. The victorious 1901 team and their supporters came home on the special train from Spilsby with the shirts draped over the engine and George Burley riding over the buffers from Firsby. There was great enthusiasm on Skegness station where the players were carried shoulder high from the platform and the local pubs were drained almost dry by kicking- out time!

Skegness United FC around 1925. Standing, left to right: Dennis Lilley (hon. sec.), Tom Coverley, Dr Fraser Menzies, Cyril Randall, Ezra Keyworth, Jack Randall, Walter Bray, Jack Parry (trainer). Seated: Edgar Lilley, Les Nicholls, 'Twister' Rowe, 'Ticker' Harland, Billy White, ? Russell.

Skegness Athletic FC grew from a YMCA youth club in the early 1920s and they became the No. 3 local team after United and Blue Rovers. Players, officials and committee members are photographed here in 1924 after winning the Skegness Hospital Challenge Cup. Standing, left to right: Jack Kime, Wilf Holland, E. Leigh, Len Fisher (trainer), Edwin Lewis, 'Snowy' Gardner, Henry Duke, George Kime, Bert Holland, ? Turner, Frank Scrafield. Middle row: Billy Miller, J. Nicholls, Jim Leech, Len Young, Horace Dexter, ? Davis. Front: Billy White, Mick Smith, Harry Fletcher, Arthur Lancaster and Ted Dimmock.

Skegness Town's Midland League side on the Burgh Road ground, March 1960. Standing left to right: Roy Walker, Malcolm Tucker, Mick Gough, Terry Webster, Tommy Lowder, Ronnie Mann, Jimmy Walker (trainer). Seated: Brian Raynor, J. Birbeck, Charlie Williams, Alick Jeffery, B. Stephens, H. Simpson. Skipper and centre half Charlie Williams was to soar to fame as a star of theatre and television, and 'wonder boy' Alick Jeffery (both signed from Doncaster Rovers) was reappearing after breaking his leg for the second time.

Skegness Youth Club footballers, known as Cosmos FC, were winners of the Lindsey Youth Clubs Cup in 1965 and the teenagers pictured here are, standing left to right: Graham Taylor, Stuart Cranidge, Chris Daniels, David Taylor, Ray Clemence, Roger Hall, Stuart Llewellyn. Kneeling: Geoff Smith, Richard Hallam, Malcolm Crowe, Ken Graham, Neil Foxon. Clemence, Daniels and Foxon soon afterwards signed for Scunthorpe and Clemence went on to keep goal for England, Liverpool and Spurs, while Foxon moved to Notts. County.

Skegness Town Football Supporters' Club setting out for a Central Alliance away fixture in March 1957. Inside the coach can be seen Walter Backhouse, Horace Johnson and Ben Topliss, with Mrs Joy Sandaver in the doorway. Outside, left to right, are: Neil Parker and Mr and Mrs Jimmy Walker and Roy and, further along, Bert Digby, Bill Storey and Phillip Hilsdon, with Les Green at the end.

Roller skating was booming in Skegness in the early 1930s when the Casino, Winter Gardens and Central Hall all became rinks. Each had its roller hockey team and they travelled as far afield as Peterborough to play matches. This is the Casino team with, back row, left to right: Sam Hayes, ? Boughton, Jack Newton, Jim Tooley, Wilf Arliss, ? McKenzie, -?-. Front: -?-, Ted Phipps, Bert Derbyshire and Ron Hewson.

SECTION FOUR
Events and Incidents

One of the earliest motor accidents in Skegness must have been this mishap in 1904, the car breaking through the fence and sliding off Roman Bank into a ditch at the bottom. A horse-drawn omnibus can be seen on its way to Ingoldmells, with the Royal Oak Hotel dimly visible on the far left. The photographer's son poses beside the empty vehicle.

When war was declared on 4 August 1914, the advance party of a contingent of Territorials had just set up camp for their annual training week in Skegness, but when the main party arrived they were immediately marched back to the railway station. This photograph of the short-lived camp in Burgh Road was taken from the old brick water tower.

Children evacuated to Skegness from Grimsby, waiting in the Tower Gardens to be collected and taken to their new homes, were photographed in September 1939 by the *Grimsby Evening Telegraph*. One wonders why Skegness was thought to be any safer than Grimsby in wartime. Note the little cardboard boxes containing the children's gas masks.

In the Second World War No 11 RAF Recruit Centre maintained a permanent staff of more than 1,100 personnel in Skegness. Hotels, guest houses and other empty premises were requisitioned and, during the four years the unit was operating, many thousands of airmen did their initial training here. This 1944 photograph of RAF Skegness Military Band shows the OC, Group Captain G.S.M. Insall VC, MC, seated centre with bandmaster Sergeant T. Simpson on his left, outside the Seacroft Hotel.

Recruits and instructors at HMS *Royal Arthur*, Butlin's Holiday Camp, in 1941.

Red Cross nurses of the First World War photographed at the former Café Dansant, Tower Esplanade.

The Skegness Red Cross Detachment at the beginning of the Second World War.

Skegness air-raid wardens in the Second World War pose outside the Grammar School. Headmaster K.G. Spendlove is seated left of centre on the front row.

Skegness Home Guard, 1940, when they were called Local Defence Volunteers (LDV), as their armbands proclaim. The first three on the back row are Bert Mastin, Cecil Chapman and Charlie Innes.

Skegness Auxiliary Fire Service members appear to be in good spirits in this snapshot, taken early in the Second World War.

Skegness and district special constables on parade outside the former police station in Ida Road in 1940.

The wartime winter of 1940/1 found Skegness cut off for three days and fifty naval recruits were seconded from HMS *Royal Arthur* (Butlin's Holiday Camp) to help dig through the five-foot snowdrifts at Croft Bank. This photograph shows F.S. Wheeler, Skegness Council's works superintendent, driving the first car through the cleared A52 in January 1941.

Summer storm, Lumley Road, on Sunday 12 July 1931. The freak squall, soon over, flooded into shops and caused a hurried evacuation of the underground lavatories as water poured down the steps. The ladies' attendant, faithful to the last, refused to abandon her post and was marooned on a table.

The annual county show, organized by the Lincolnshire Agricultural Society, moved to a different town each year until a permanent site near Lincoln came into use in 1959. The show was held at Skegness in 1912, 1922 and 1930 and these photographs show gaily decorated Lumley Square at the 1922 event. Ornamental arches were erected at the entrances to Lumley Road and Richmond Drive, with banners proclaiming 'Success to Agriculture' and 'God Speed the Plough'. The showground in Richmond Drive occupied 25 acres and the total attendance over the two days was 22,598. Several omnibuses can be seen in these photographs, including the Progressive open-top double-decker which ran a regular service between Skegness and Boston. These snapshots were taken by the young daughter (now Mrs M.A. Dykes) of James Barlow, the grocer, whose shop can be seen in the top picture. As a footnote, the 1912 county show at Skegness was nearly cancelled because of a foot-and-mouth standstill order which came into force when animals were already on the road. The show went on, but the only livestock exhibited were Irish cattle which had arrived a day earlier.

Battle of Flowers, Skegness.

The Battle of Flowers, in the 1890s and later, was Skegness's carnival time, and Lumley Road and the parades were garlanded with flags and flowers. This procession passing the Clock Tower was around 1905, but the lower photograph shows an earlier cavalcade at almost the same spot, before the Clock Tower was erected in 1898/9. Note also that the public shelter on Grand Parade had not been built at the earlier date.

Crowds gather at the entrance to Lumley Road to watch the 1905 Battle of Flowers procession go by. The chap who lettered the banner appears to have had difficulty with the 'N'.

In the same place, around 1921, this carnival procession passes under a mock medieval archway in Lumley Road, headed by a band and the lifeboat, the crew in oilskins and life-jackets.

A guard of honour preceeding Princess Marie Louise of Schleswig-Holstein – on foot with her attendant ladies, all in large hats – on their way to lay the foundation stone of Skegness Cottage Hospital on 29 September 1911. The princess was a grand daughter of Queen Victoria and daughter of Princess Christian of Schleswig-Holstein. She was a close friend of the wife of Captain (later Sir Archibald) Weigall, the local MP, both of whom accompanied her on this occasion. Mrs Weigall's first husband had been Baron von Eckardstein and she was able to produce the German 'royal' for special occasions in her second husband's constituency. Two years after the Skegness ceremony, Princess Marie Louise carried out the official opening of Wainfleet's Coronation Hall.

Butlin's grand carnival procession, 1933, headed by Billy B. himself, standing in the leading car. Seventy brass bands followed, competing in the great band contest at the camp that weekend.

By the early 1920s there were a number of motorized turnouts in the processions, and Dutton's Cash Stores entered this gondola on wheels, photographed outside the cricket ground in 1922. Gertie, young Peter and Connie Dutton are to the right of the lady at the steering wheel, while Cllr Reginald Dutton gives the entry a final once-over from the pavement. Peter Dutton was killed piloting a bomber in the raid on Eindhoven in December 1942.

But what has happened right in front of St Matthew's church? This carnival horse appears to have slipped down and the men try desperately to avoid flying hoofs and get the poor animal back on its feet.

Maypole dancers under instruction in 1910, and (below) young dancers at the Children's Pageant in the Tower Gardens, 1923. The latter appear to have a little more leg freedom than their predecessors.

Skegness Amateur Operatic Society's staging of *The Mikado* in 1924 featured Messrs Leslie, Boulton and Stokley in the parts of Pish-Tush, Ko-Ko and Pooh-Bah respectively. Left: Mr Boulton goes down on his knees to Miss Madge Walker.

Skegness Amateur Operatic Society presented *The Chocolate Soldier* to a packed audience at Arcadia Theatre in April 1937, starring Phyllis Wright, James Leslie, Jack Huntridge, Gwen Chapman and Lily Crane. This was the full company, with musical director, W. Edwin Furniss, on the far left. The producer was Walter J. Fearn.

Skegness Amateur Dramatic Society's annual production in March 1933 was *Third Time Lucky*, staged at the Arcadia Theatre. Left to right in this tense scene are: Evelyn Lill, Jack Marshall, John Nelson and Stanley Hall. The producer was Gertrude Huggins, afterwards Mrs John Nelson.

HRH Princes Margaret has a smile for the guard of honour formed by the Skegness Girl Guides, with District Commissioner Mary Wheatley at their head, outside the Town Hall on 28 May 1968. The Princess later visited Natureland and took a boat trip along the Waterway. Afterwards she attended a Church of England youth conference at Butlin's Camp.

Deputy Chief Scout Sir Percy Everitt in 1936 officially declared open St George's Hall, Wainfleet Road, the new headquarters of the Skegness Scouts and Girl Guides. Left to right: Skegness Scoutmaster Jim Crawshaw, County Commissioner Capt. J.S. Reeve (Leadenham), District Commissioner Mrs E.E. Jackson (Skegness), Sir Percy Everitt County Commissioner, Mrs W.H. Rawnsley (Well Vale), Assistant District Commissioner Capt. C.E. Jay (Alford), District Commissioner Capt. C.C. Eiffe (Skegness), and Assistant County Commissioner Mrs Boys (Woodhall Spa).

HRH The Duchess of Gloucester opened the new maternity wing and other extensions at Skegness & District Hospital on 25 May 1939, when she accepted donations towards the cost of the work from more than 150 local children. Here, little Brenda Simpson of Addlethorpe is being gently ushered before the Duchess to hand over her purse by Miss Dianah Stow. Sir Archibald Weigall, former MP for the Horncastle Division, is seated on the right, with Lady Weigall partly visible.

Skegness & District Hospital was honoured by a visit from the Rt Hon. Enoch Powell, Minister of Health, on 21 June 1962. He is seen here examining the new coin-operated telephone trolley, with hospital secretary Arthur Dearden and matron, Mrs J.M. Bennett.

Edward Steere (left), a Londoner, came to Skegness in 1858 to act as curate and also assist the vicar of Burgh-with-Winthorpe, the Revd William Tozer (right). In 1862 Tozer became Bishop of Central Africa, moving to Zanzibar, and shortly afterwards he invited Steere to join him. By that time, the latter had moved to Little Steeping as vicar, but he eagerly answered the call to the Dark Continent and, when the ex-vicar of Burgh-le-Marsh was forced to resign through ill health in 1874, Steere was appointed bishop. His missionary journeys took him hundreds of miles on foot in the difficult and often hostile terrain of Nyasaland, and in Zanzibar he built a cathedral on the site of the old slave market. Worn out and sick, the former Skegness curate died in his jungle diocese in 1882, aged fifty-four, and was buried in his cathedral.

Remembrance Sunday, 1953, with Cllr Elsa Barratt, chairman of the Skegness Urban District Council, placing a wreath on the town war memorial. Far left is vice-chairman Cllr Alfred Denham and, centre, town clerk Ivor M. Cule. The Rectory can be seen in the background in this *Skegness Standard* picture.

The proclamation of Queen Elizabeth's accession to the throne was read out from the Town Hall balcony by Skegness UDC chairman, Cllr George Swaby, in May 1952. The former Town Hall faced Roman Bank on the corner of Algitha Road and was demolished in 1966 after the Council had moved to North Parade. Photographed by the *Skegness Standard*.

The lifeboat *Anne Allen* on service in an ice-bound sea in February 1947, searching for the missing Dutch vessel *Tuko*. The anchored ship was located, but refused assistance. Left to right: Hedley Grunnill, Bill Perrin, Harold Steel and Lance Grunnill.

On lifeboat flag days in the earlier part of this century the lifeboat would give a life-saving demonstration at high tide, with the Pier forming a grandstand and hundreds of other spectators crowding the water's edge.

Four Skegness boatmen joined together to purchase and operate the former Coverack lifeboat, renamed *Grace Darling II*. This 1935 photograph shows the boat heavily loaded and low down in the water after taking passengers off the local pleasure cruiser, *Elizabeth Allan*, when the latter caught fire. The cruiser was not severely damaged, but the passengers were transferred to the former lifeboat as a precautionary measure. Skipper George Perrin can be seen in the stern as the boat floats at anchor, waiting for the passengers to be taken ashore. The plaque near the prow tells us that the former Cornwall lifeboat saved ninety-eight lives, and although the people on board on this occasion were not actually in very great peril, the *Grace Darling II* afterwards rescued two holidaymakers blown out to sea in a sinking boat, to bring her tally to a full century.

The ex-naval patrol boat *Helen* had been brought to Skegness in August 1932 to convert to a pleasure boat, but it was so badly damaged after running aground it was never used. The owner subsequently replaced it with the cruiser *Elizabeth Allan*.

It was a warm, sunny morning on 8 July 1893 when the Skegness pleasure boat *Shannon*, with nearly thirty holidaymakers aboard, sailed into the Wash. Half an hour later the sky had clouded over and as *Shannon* made for home a gale sprang up with thunder and lightning and a deluge of rain. Skipper Edward Grunnill and his mate and cousin, Edwin Grunnill, rushed to haul in the sail as the yawl dipped and rose in the surging sea, a mile or so off Gibraltar Point. Then a crashing gust shattered the mast, the boat listed in the trough, turned over and disappeared under the waves.

A few hundred yards away, Jabez Grunnill was fishing in his little boat, *Dart*, and he would have suffered the same fate had he not been drifting without sail. The squall subsided as suddenly as it had sprung up and Jabez searched for survivors. He hauled three exhausted men aboard but the rest were drowned, including the skipper and mate. The twenty-eight victims were mostly London railway employees and their families who had come to Skegness for their annual day outing. Pictured is Jabez Grunnill and the silver medal presented to him 'by a few friends', as it is inscribed on the reverse.

The cargo schooner *Europa*, of Amsterdam, anchored almost opposite the Sea View Hotel to ride out the storm of 20 March 1919. Skegness lifeboat coxswain, Matthew Grunnill, twice warned the skipper that the morning tide could carry him into the Pier but he refused to believe that he was in danger. About 8 o'clock next day, *Europa*, dragging her anchor, crashed into the Pier stern first, inflicting great damage to both the structure and the ship. Lifeboat crewmen and other helpers were already on the pier decking, marshalled by Matt Grunnill, and ropes were dropped to haul the Dutchmen to safety. The vessel grounded on the falling tide and was eventually towed by tug to Grimsby for extensive refitting. A temporary walkway bridged the gap in the pier, but a permanent repair was not effected until twenty years later. The photographs were taken by C.J. Farmer.

Skegness escaped without loss of life in the great East Coast Flood on the night of 31 January 1953 but the foreshore installations were inundated, with much material damage. As shown above, the water reached up to Grand Parade – stayed by the parade wall built in the 1870's – leaving the meteorological screen isolated.

The sea flooded over the bowling greens and gardens and surrounded the Sun Castle, causing much interior damage. In the vicinity of Butlin's Holiday Camp, in Ingoldmells parish, sixteen lives were lost and the sea walls were ripped apart all the way to Mablethorpe.

For almost a century Skegness Pier was the dominating feature of the seashore, but dooms-night arrived on 11 January 1978. The high spring tide, combined with a northerly gale, breached the Pier in two places, leaving the pierhead and the section carrying the two shelters as tall offshore islands. The shelters with their substructure were removed in 1984, and the following autumn the demolition of the pierhead began. On Saturday 27 October 1985 workmen left an incinerator unattended and a spark ignited nearby woodwork, setting the whole place ablaze. By morning, the pierhead was a blackened iron skeleton (below) and the last rites were just a formality.

The destruction of Skegness Pier in the night-time storm of 11 January 1978 is vividly captured in this classic photograph by Jim Stuart.

His other photograph, a happier event in the same area, slickly captures the moment of the Red Arrows' head-on spectacular during one of their displays in the 1970s. This was taken from the north side of the Pier.

Aviator B.C. Hucks gave flying exhibitions in a number of Lincolnshire towns in 1913, and at Skegness on 26–8 June he flew his 70 h.p Bleriot monoplane from the showground field, now the Richmond car park. Hucks is credited with being the first Briton to loop the loop. He was a test pilot in the war soon to follow, but he died in the great influenza epidemic of 1919.

Two competitors in the Skegness Motor Races of 1924. Motor racing had taken place on the sands as early as 1905 and was revived in 1923 on a course opposite Seacroft. The following summer the meeting attracted such notable entries as G.E.T. Eyston's Aston-Martin, Raymond Mays' Brescia-Bugatti, S.F. Edge's AC, Capt. Malcolm Campbell's Sunbeam Bluebird, Parry Thomas' Leyland-Thomas and Ivy Cummings' Frazer-Nash. Reginald Dutton was the meeting secretary, Tom Cary chief marshal and Cllr C.T. Jessap chairman of the executive committee.

Horse racing on the central beach in the early 1920s, with spectators crowding the sand-hills and the Café Dansant visible in the distance. Races had been held as far back as 1829 but they were not revived until fifty years later, when the 1879 course was opposite the Sea View Hotel.

Greyhound races were staged at Burgh Road in the early 1930s, shown here with the newly-built Lumley School not far away. The 'hare' was a rabbitskin tied to a rope wound up on a windlass, but it appears to have stimulated the runners to great effort.

Seacroft Golf Links was declared open by the Earl of Scarbrough on 23 April 1895 and here, on the right, he can be seen driving off the first tee. It will be observed that this came almost up to the Vine Hotel, but it was moved further south in 1900 when the course was extended from nine to eighteen holes.

The last stroke of a match on the Seacroft links, on 24 August 1907, between Arnaud Massy and the legendary J.H. Taylor.

When the North Shore Golf Links, at the other end of the town, was officially opened on 25 April 1910, local MP, Lord Willoughby de Eresby, drove off the first ball. This was followed by a match between four British Open winners, James Braid (5 times), J.H. Taylor (5), Harry Vardon (6) and George Duncan (1), seen here facing the camera. There were a thousand guests at the reception, including the Lord Mayor of Nottingham.

The Skegness Old Folks' Treat was an annual tea and entertainment instituted in 1887 to mark Queen Victoria's Golden Jubilee. George J. Crofts became the guiding spirit, assisted by a number of local business people, and a minstrel concert featured on several occasions. Our picture shows the cast of a play called *The New Boy*, performed around the time of the First World War. Standing, left to right: Mrs Kathleen Frith, J.E. Middleton, Fred Crofts in the title role, George C. Dunkley, R.J.G. Dutton, Harry Frith, Miss Ada Crofts, -?-. Seated: G.J. Crofts as the schoolmaster and Miss Mollie Dunkley. The play was performed in the King's Theatre and tea was served in the Tower Gardens Pavilion. After Mr Crofts died his daughter carried on the tradition until the function had to be discontinued in 1937.

Billy Rowe's Buffet was a popular jugs-of-tea stall at the bottom of Tower Esplanade in the 1920s and '30s, but near the end of the Second World War the Urban District Council decided to take over all the foreshore catering establishments, causing a loud outcry among the tenants. When Billy Rowe's eldest son, Reuben, returned from six years' soldiering in 1945 and found the family business confiscated, he decided to go into battle again. The first post-war council election attracted thirty-two candidates for ten seats and Reuben only just missed topping the poll. He campaigned hard to reprivatize the refreshment places and four years later, when the council-run cafés were losing money, he missed reversing the policy by only one vote. Billy Rowe's Buffet never got back on the sands.

The summertime sensation of 1937, as far as Skegness was concerned, was the death in a lions' cage of the notorious ex-rector of Stiffkey, a village on the Norfolk coast. Convicted by a Church House Consistory Court of immoral conduct with London prostitutes, Harold Davidson began a bizarre campaign to clear his character, culminating in a publicity act in Fred Rye's sideshow in the North Parade amusement park. On the evening of 28 July 1937, after delivering his usual discourse, the ex-rector was treading round the cage behind the two lions when one of them turned round and attacked him. Badly mauled and unconscious, he was rushed to Skegness Hospital where he died two days later. The photograph shows the diminutive Mr Davidson being welcomed by Fred Rye (who bred lions at his Poplar Farm, near Burgh) and Renee Somner, the lion trainer who went to his assistance, belabouring the lion on the head with her whipstock.

Acknowledgements

The author is grateful for the loan of postcards and photographs from the following, used in addition to the illustrations from his own collection:

Norman Barker • John Berry • Hedley Cook • John Cowpe • Miss Betty Dutton
Ken Epton • Mrs Dorothy Farrar • Tony Fisher • Stanley Fravigar
Mick French • Walter Girling • *Grimsby Evening Telegraph* • Ben Hancock
Mrs C. Hewson • Ken Holland BEM • Mrs Claudia Kirk • Miss Evelyn M. Lill
Basil Major • Mrs Cecy Mastin • Miss Barbara Neale • William Nelson
Charles North • Archer Osbourne • Frank Parkins • Dennis Plant
Michael Richards • Fred Sellars • Mrs Ivy Simpson • Skegness County Library
Skegness Standard • Miss Mary Wheatley • Henry Wilkinson • Tony Wood